Sold on Selling:
Skills and Techniques

Doug Malouf

American Media Publishing

4900 University Avenue
West Des Moines, IA 50266-6769
800-262-2557

Sold on Selling: *Skills and Techniques*

Doug Malouf

This publication is designed to provide accurate and authoritative information in regard to the subject matter covered. It is sold with the understanding that neither the author nor the publisher is engaged in rendering legal, accounting, or other professional service. If legal advice or other expert assistance is required, the services of a competent professional person should be sought.

Credits:

American Media Publishing:	Arthur Bauer
	Todd McDonald
	Gayle Stockberger
Project Manager:	Esther Vanier
Designer:	Janet Ferguson Dooley

Published by American Media, Inc., 4900 University Avenue, West Des Moines, IA 50266-6769
First Edition

Library of Congress Catalog Card Number 96-84567
Malouf, Doug
Sold on Selling: Skills and Techniques

Printed in the United States of America
ISBN 1-884926-54-1

The AMI How-To Series

To obtain information about these and other AMI How-To Series books, please call American Media Publishing at **800-262-2557.**

TITLE	PRICE	QUANTITY	TOTAL
The Art of Giving and Receiving Feedback Shirley Poertner & Karen Massetti Miller	$12.95/ea.		
Assertiveness Skills Nelda Shelton and Sharon Burton	$12.95/ea.		
Attitude: The Choice Is Yours Michele Matt Yanna	$12.95/ea.		
Customer Service Excellence Debra J. MacNeill	$12.95/ea.		
Documenting Discipline Mike Deblieux	$12.95/ea.		
Effective Delegation Skills Bruce B. Tepper	$12.95/ea.		
Effective Teamwork Michael D. Maginn	$12.95/ea.		
High Impact Presentations Robert W. Pike, CSP	$14.95/ea.		
The Human Touch Performance Appraisal Charles M. Cadwell	$12.95/ea.		
I Have to Fire Someone! Richard S. Deems, Ph.D.	$12.95/ea.		
Interviewing: More Than A Gut Feeling Richard S. Deems, Ph.D.	$12.95/ea.		
Investing Time for Maximum Return Melody Mackenzie and Alec Mackenzie	$12.95/ea.		
Leading Teams: The Skills For Success Sam R. Lloyd	$12.95/ea.		
Listen Up: Hear What's Really Being Said Jim Dugger	$12.95/ea.		
Job Strategies for New Employees Robert W. Lucas	$12.95/ea.		
Making Change Work For You! Richard S. Deems, Ph.D.	$12.95/ea.		
Making Meetings Work Karen Anderson	$12.95/ea.		
Managing Conflict at Work Jim Murphy	$12.95/ea.		
Managing Stress Kristine C. Brewer	$12.95/ea.		
Negotiate With Confidence Ed Brodow	$12.95/ea.		
The New Supervisor: Skills for Success Bruce B. Tepper	$12.95/ea.		
Positive Mental Attitude in the Workplace Marian Thomas	$12.95/ea.		
Self-Esteem: The Power to Be Your Best Marc Towers	$12.95/ea.		
Sold on Selling: Skills and Techniques Doug Malouf	$12.95/ea.		
Ten Tools for Quality Richard Chang, Ph.D.	$12.95/ea.		
Training That Works! Charles M. Cadwell	$12.95/ea.		
Writing for Business Results Patricia E. Seraydarian	$12.95/ea.		
Shipping and handling will be added to your order.	**TOTAL**		

Four Easy Ways To Order

☎ **CALL:** 800-262-2557

📠 **FAX:** 515-224-0256

✉ **MAIL:** American Media Incorporated
4900 University Avenue
West Des Moines,
Iowa 50266-6769

🖥 **E-MAIL:** AMI@ammedia.com

Name _____

Title _____

Organization _____

Address _____

City _____

State/Zip _____

Daytime Phone (_____) _____

FAX _____

Method of Payment

☐ I've enclosed check #_____
  payable to American Media Inc.

☐ Credit Card — Charge my order,
plus shipping and handling to my credit card.

☐ Mastercard   ☐ VISA   ☐ American Express

MasterCard   VISA   AMERICAN EXPRESS

Exp. Date | MO. | YR. |

CARD NO.

☐☐☐☐ - ☐☐☐☐ - ☐☐☐☐ - ☐☐☐☐

Signature _____

This page is reproducible
for easy reference and faxing.

About the Author

Doug Malouf is an international professional speaker. His business seminars travel the world. This is the third book that he has published in the U.S.A. His practical approach to selling comes from his background. At the age of 7, he was selling horseshoe nails, Jello, butter, and tea in his father's general store and from those early years has built a business network. A regular visitor to the U.S.A., he has received professional contribution awards from the American Society for Training and Development and has been a keynote presenter at their international conference for ten consecutive years. He is one of Australia's most respected sales trainers who crisscrosses America with his unique interactive presentation skills style. He has appeared on R.E.T.N. Cable Television and visits the U.S. every May and September for business seminars.

He can be contacted at Dougmal Training Systems, 6 Flinders Street, North Wollongong, Australia 2500. Telephone (61) 42 26 2111; Facsimile (61) 42 27 2545.

Introduction

Selling is a basic part of life for all of us. It's a bit like love. Remember the old saying: "Love makes the world go 'round"? Well, I also believe that selling makes the world go 'round. This book will show beginners how to jump on the carousel, experienced sellers how to stay there, and all sales professionals how to have fun at the same time.

Selling has come into its own. It is no longer the job you do when you don't have a job. It's a job you do because you enjoy it. It's a job that requires you to develop and maintain professional knowledge and skills. And if you want to be a really high-performance salesperson, it's a job you have to be proud of and genuinely enjoy. You also have to strive to keep learning so that you become acknowledged as an expert in your chosen field.

The essential thing about selling is that it is a people business. It focuses on communication. Today's seller is:

- Genuinely interested in people.
- A good listener rather than a good talker—a listener who encourages people to talk honestly about their needs and problems.
- An empathetic person who can look at the sale from the buyer's point of view.
- Adept at "reading" other people's personal styles of communication and reacting appropriately.
- Good at gathering information and using it to help people to satisfy their needs and solve their problems.

The skills of the salesperson are very similar to the skills possessed by other professionals—essentially, communication skills. So remember this basic lesson as you read through this book: selling isn't something you do to people, it's something you do with people, through effective communication and sensitive interaction. Selling also isn't something you can learn how to do in one intensive lesson. If you want to stay on top in sales, you never stop learning. This book will give you new insights to add to your current store of knowledge.

CHAPTER ONE

Sales Success in Nine Easy Steps

Chapter Objectives

This chapter will help you to:

☑ Identify the nine steps in the Sales Cycle.

☑ Recognize your own strengths and weaknesses at each step of the Sales Cycle.

Where Are You Now?

I don't know you. I don't know whether you are new to the art of selling, or whether you've been around a while. You could be just scratching out an existence, or you could be on your way to being a millionaire.

One thing I do know: if you're reading this book, you're a professional. You're committed to learning, and that's a good thing.

The most successful men and women I know never stop learning. They say things like: *"I always read the latest books on selling because even if I pick up just one new tip, it's worthwhile."* They go to seminars. They network. They learn as much as they can about people: what makes them laugh, what makes them cry, what makes them angry. ***And, what makes them buy.***

The Sales Cycle

The nine steps in the Sales Cycle have been around for a long, long time. The sales cycle has gone by a lot of different names, as fads come and go, but it's always been there.

Those nine easy steps to your sales success are:

1. Organizing your record keeping and work habits.

2. Prospecting for customers.

3. Building rapport with prospects.

4. Exploring customers' needs.

5. Presenting your product effectively.

6. Handling customers' objections.

7. Testing customers' reactions during the sale.

8. Closing the sale.

9. Delivering outstanding after-sales service.

Are you nodding your head as you read this, thinking, "Well, everything there is common sense, really"? If you are, that's as it should be. It *should* seem practical and logical.

Now let me ask you this: if it's all so logical and practical, why aren't more sales professionals getting it right? Why are so many sellers out there just eking out an existence? Why don't their incomes reflect their understanding of the process?

Simple—they understand the process, but they don't *do* it. They may *think* they follow all the steps, but they don't. And a simple self-check would show that.

Self-Check: Nine Steps to Sales Success

Take this simple quiz now. It will show you exactly what you're forgetting to do, or didn't know you should do, or didn't think you had time to do. This is where you start, no matter how long you've been in selling.

In each of the 9 sections of the quiz, rate your ability between 1 and 10. The closer to 10 you are, the better you are. Be honest. Underneath the continuum from 1-10, there's a space for you to justify the rating you've given yourself.

1. How organized are you?

Explain why you've given yourself the above rating.

_____

_____

2. How good are you at prospecting for new business?

Account for your success or lack of success in prospecting.

_____

_____

3. How would you judge your ability to establish rapport with people?

1   2   3   4   5   6   7   8   9   10

Account for your level of success or lack of success at establishing

rapport._____

_____

_____

4. How skilled are you at exploring the client's needs, wants, and buying power?

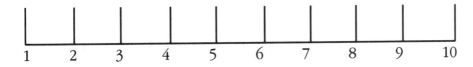

1   2   3   4   5   6   7   8   9   10

I give myself the above rating because _____

_____

_____.

5. How would you rate your presentation skills?

1   2   3   4   5   6   7   8   9   10

I give myself the above rating because _____

_____

_____.

6. How adept are you at handling questions and objections?

1   2   3   4   5   6   7   8   9   10

Outline your standard procedure for handling objections. _____

_____

_____

7. How skilled are you at monitoring customers' reactions throughout the sales process?

1   2   3   4   5   6   7   8   9   10

Outline your strategy for tracking a client's response throughout the

sales process. _____

_____

_____

8. How would you rate your success at getting the sale?

1   2   3   4   5   6   7   8   9   10

Describe your methods in closing a sale. _____

_____

_____

9. Rate the quality of your after-sales service:

What do you feel you do to ensure quality after-sales service?

_____

_____

_____

Chapter Summary

No matter where you are in the sales hierarchy, you should be asking yourself: how can I improve? As you work your way through each section of this book, look back at your answers to this quiz. See if your perceptions and ideas change. Ask constantly, *What else could I do? What new insights can I add to the selling process?* And perhaps the most important thing of all, *What of value can I pass on to others?*

CHAPTER TWO

Step 1: Organizing Your Record Keeping and Work Habits

Chapter Objectives

This chapter will help you to:

☑ Streamline your record keeping.

☑ Organize your product knowledge by using the Q&A approach.

☑ Identify the essentials of time management.

Become Absolutely Organized

In any profession, the organized person has the greatest chance of success. In selling, organization is essential. If you are organized, you:

- Have up-to-date product knowledge at your fingertips.
- Know what to say to a customer at any stage of the sales cycle.
- Know how to manage your time to achieve the best results in your working day.
- Can instantly locate any information you need.

Streamline Your Record Keeping

The way you organize yourself and your day will depend on the type of selling you do. If you are a sales assistant in a store, you might find it more convenient to keep your records in loose-leaf folders and a pocket diary. If you spend some of your time at a desk, a desktop computer might work well. Sales reps who are constantly on the road often like to use a laptop computer and a portable printer.

Perhaps a combination of the above will work for you, such as a desktop computer plus a small loose-leaf diary. Whatever the organizational method you choose, make sure it facilitates:

- Effective management of your time;
- Ready access to information; and
- Prompt relay of messages.

Take a Moment...

Become Super Organized
Write down 3 things you will do immediately to become more organized.

1. _____

_____

_____

2. _____

_____

_____

3. _____

_____

_____

2

Update Your Product Information

Some people spend a lot of time maintaining customer records but very little time developing and updating their product knowledge. This is a big mistake no matter how long you've been selling.

Revision of product knowledge is something that "old hands" in particular tend to let slide. They've been in the game a while, and they're fairly certain they know all the strategies. They think they can bluff their way through without having to spend too much time keeping their product knowledge up to date.

They're wrong. Customers can smell a bluff at twenty paces. Try to con them, and they'll be turned off both you and the purchase. Why should they place any trust in someone who obviously doesn't know the product? Why should they believe your claims that it's a good buy?

Take a moment to see where you stand on product knowledge. Is there any way you can improve your understanding of your products?

Take a Moment...

Know Your Product

Do this now: Mentally review your knowledge of goods and services in your business. Complete this sentence.

I should probably update my product knowledge on...

_____

_____

_____

_____

The Q&A Approach to Product Knowledge

A sound knowledge of the product will build your confidence and translate into more sales. Here's an idea that will help you pull into the fast lane.

☑ Divide a piece of paper into two columns. For the next thirty days, write every question someone asks you about your product in the left-hand column. At the end of each day, review your list. Find out the answers to any questions you were unable to answer and write them in the right-hand column.

We call this technique the *Q&A Approach to Product Knowledge.*

Let's see how the Q&A Approach works with a customer. Suppose someone says to you: "How long will this computer take to process the data?" Your answer is not "I don't know." That answer destroys your credibility in a matter of seconds. Instead, you say, "May I check that and get back to you, please?"

Next, enter the question into your question column. Find out the answer, record it, and call your customer with the information. Repeat the process for each new question you receive, and after thirty days, your product knowledge will have increased dramatically. After the first thirty days, you should review your sheet every week.

The Q&A Approach increases both your knowledge and your effectiveness. There are two messages in this for any sales professional:

1. To sell more we need to increase our face-to-face contact.

2. To increase our effectiveness we need an error-correction technique.

The Error Correction Review

At the end of each day take ten minutes to relax, then open your Q&A Approach diary and draw a line across the bottom of that day's page. Ask yourself, *If I had today to live over again, how could I have been more effective?* Jot down your response(s).

If you adopt this idea, you'll find that each day is a "lesson" day. If you missed a sale because you were late, the Error Correction Review (ECR) will show: DON'T BE LATE. Then you can develop a plan that will let you put your observations into action.

Improve Your Time Management

The way you spend your time has a direct influence on how much money you earn. If you waste time, you waste money. To be sure you haven't wasted your time, you need to be able to justify the way you have spent it.

By adopting effective time management techniques, you can maximize your effectiveness in selling. We can't change the number of hours in a day, but we *can* change our work habits.

As you engage in each new activity in your working day, ask yourself these questions:

- Is this profitable?
- Is this necessary?
- Could I have delegated this?

If you get a string of NOs under "Is this profitable?" and "Is this necessary?" you have time management problems.

"By adopting effective time management techniques, you can maximize your effectiveness in selling."

Take a Moment...

Let's Get Organized

Write down details of how you organize the following aspects of your day.

Customer Records _____

_____

_____

Product Knowledge _____

_____

_____

Things To Do _____

_____

_____

Customer Follow-up _____

_____

_____

2

Planning Your Time Effectively

To plan your time effectively, you must establish both goals and priorities. The best way to set goals is to write a daily "To-Do" list, then rank those tasks in order of importance, employing four categories of time use:

Class A Time = Face-to-face contact with a buyer or seller. It involves two people who can make decisions.

Class B Time = Time spent preparing to use Class A time (product knowledge, preparation of presentations, etc.).

Class C Time = Other administrative/work activities such as writing ads, preparing stock lists, waiting to speak to clients, or stocking shelves.

Class D Time = Time spent in ways not directly related to work, such as coffee breaks or casual conversation.

Include a *Priorities* column to the right of your daily To-Do list. Next to each activity you have listed, mark a 1, 2, or 3 in the Priorities column:

1 = Must Do;   2 = Should Do;   3 = Could Do.

Make out your list at the beginning of your day or even the night before. List your activities and allocate priorities. Then ask yourself, "How can I allocate my time according to the priorities I have set?" This will force you to plan specifically for each day's work.

As the day progresses, check your activities regularly. Ask yourself, "Is this what I planned to do?" and "Is this the best use of my time just now?"

Remember, you don't need to give priority to Class A activities at all times. Other types of activities are important too. Establish a balance between the different types of activities that will be most productive for you. That balance should:

- Ensure that Class A activities are given enough time to allow you to achieve a high rate of sales.

- Reduce to a minimum time spent on activities that are not related to sales in any way.

Chapter Summary

☑ Organized people have greater success in selling.

☑ Make sure your system facilitates effective management of your time, ready access to information, and prompt relay of messages.

☑ A sound knowledge of your product will build your confidence and translate into more sales.

☑ A daily Error Correction Review will increase your effectiveness as a seller.

☑ As you engage in each new activity in your working day, ask yourself:

- Is this profitable?
- Is this necessary?
- Could I have delegated this?

☑ Prepare a daily To-Do list and prioritize your tasks.

CHAPTER THREE

Step 2: Prospecting for Customers

Chapter Objectives

This chapter will help you to:

☑ Design a prospecting plan.

☑ Map your personal network.

☑ Learn how to project a positive company image.

Your Prospecting Plan

If your business isn't growing, there's a good chance it's in the early stages of decay. The cure for that is to develop a well-organized attack and seek out new business opportunities that will help your company prosper and grow. In other words, think about developing an ***effective approach to prospecting***.

Use this 3-A guide to business growth:

1. ***Awareness:*** The potential buyer has to know who you are and what you sell.

2. ***Accessibility:*** You have to be easy to find and easy to deal with. (Some people are easy to find and hard to do business with.)

3. ***Approval:*** The approval of the individual buyer and the business community at large is the surest base for continued growth. A good reputation is your most valuable business asset.

Build Your Personal Network

Leave Business Cards

Your network has to reach out into every area of your daily life. Your hairdresser, your accountant, your mechanic, and your grocer can all help you to make sales. Give them a stack of business cards. Make sure the cards show clearly *who you are, what you sell*, and *where to find you*.

Distribute Company Gifts

Pens, desk calendars, and key rings will remind people of your company every time they write a note or start their cars. Each item should display your company name and telephone number.

Use Letterhead for All Your Correspondence

Whenever you write a letter, make sure that it's on attractively designed letterhead. Your company name and address, your own name, and a contact telephone number should be clearly displayed at the top of each page.

"Whenever you write a letter, make sure that it's on attractively designed letterhead."

3

Take a Moment...

Analyze your personal network

To find new prospects, I could contact or leave cards with the following people.

Family _____

_____

Friends _____

_____

Businesses I Patronize (e.g. mechanic, hairdresser) _____

_____

Business Acquaintances _____

_____

Sports Teams/Social Clubs _____

_____

Other _____

_____

Set Up a Client Contact System

People like to be remembered. They appreciate it when you recall their names and some personal details. You can record this information in a number of ways: with a simple card system, with an electronic organizer, or on a computer database that prints out whatever you need when you need it. Use whichever system works best for you.

Let's review the essentials of a client contact system. As you will see, it's basically common sense. You probably have something like it operating already. If not—you have some work to do!

- Whenever you meet someone new, make a special effort to remember the details of most importance: his or her name, spouse's name, number of children, and interests. Record those details as soon as possible.

- If that person becomes a client, use the information to remind you of details that will personalize your contact with him or her.

- Record what you talk about each time you make contact.

Client Contact Systems in the Information Age

There are a host of excellent computer programs available to help you keep track of clients. They range from simple PIMs (Personal Information Managers) to heavy-duty contact managers that will record contact details, company history, and all-in-one phone operations.

As programs become more sophisticated, there's very little difference between a good PIM and a basic contact manager. Essentially, PIMs organize information (appointments, events, people, tasks) in an easily accessible format. Contact managers place more emphasis on keeping track of people and producing reports for sales and marketing. You'll probably be familiar with names such as Daytimer, Lotus Organizer, Tracker, and ACT!. These are just a few of the many excellent products available. Ask dealers for product reviews to determine which one will best suit your needs.

How do you choose a PIM or contact manager that will work for you? Look for:

- **Ease of use.** Information must be easily and quickly accessible. The whole idea is to save you time.
- **Pop-up menus** and an **on-line help feature**.
- **Group capabilities** if you work as part of a sales team.
- **A search engine** to help you find information fast.

Some questions to ask yourself before you go shopping:

- Do I want e-mail capability?
- Do I want to print out hard copy to use in a paper-based organizer?
- Do I want to print out sales reports and forecasts?

Be Visible in the Marketplace

The most obvious way to be visible is to advertise. Use the local newspapers and radio stations and the yellow pages. You can also arrange media coverage about your local business, you can run workshops offering free (or cheap) advice, and you can ask for a newspaper or radio interview if you publish a book or a helpful booklet. Remember, today's sellers are **proactive**, not **reactive**. You have to be visible and so does your product.

Pre-call Planning

There are three basic types of prospecting calls:

- **Cold calls**—You don't know them; they don't know you.
- **Warm calls**—You know them; they don't want you.
- **Hot calls**—They know you, they trust you, and they have a need.

> **"Today's sellers are *proactive*, not *reactive*. You have to be visible and so does your product."**

Not many of us like being in the "cold call" situation. There's no trust, no rapport, and the prospect is likely to be suspicious of you. That's where pre-call planning comes in.

Pre-call planning puts you in the classification of "warm to hot." It simply means doing your homework before you call on the prospect. This type of call puts you in control, and it's more cost-effective because there's more chance of a positive result.

Information about your prospect can come from:
- The media.
- Personal friends or business contacts.
- New businesses openings and directories.
- Telephone books.
- Keeping your eyes and ears open.

Pre-call planning allows you to control your time with a particular prospect. If used effectively:

- *You* decide before the call if you want the business.
- *You* control your time.
- *You* make the moves to open the account.
- *You* use persistence to get the account.

3

The Seven Steps to Pre-call Planning

1. **Identify the target prospects.** Is this the business you want?

2. **Research their position.** Will this be a good account? Who are the decision-makers?

3. **Make contact.** Telephone to set up your appointment. At this stage you're still not selling.

4. **Build rapport—just open the door.** Don't sell the product, sell yourself. Keep this first appointment short.

5. **Explore the DBM.** Find out their Dominant Buying Motive. What are their needs?

6. **Plan your presentation around the DBM.** Plan your presentation around their needs.

7. **Knock it over!** Test your information, then close.

How to Make More "Hot" Calls Than "Cold" Calls

It's easier to sell to an established customer than find a new one. It's been proven over and over again. To make your job easier, all you have to do is hold on to those established clients. Ensure their loyalty, and presto! You're making far more "hot" calls (to people who know you and trust you) than cold calls (which we all hate).

It always seems to come down to trust. For your customers to stay loyal, they have to believe that you're watching out for their interests. To make sure those clients don't forget you, it's essential that you stay in contact—not so much that you become a nuisance, just enough so they remember you.

Listen to your clients' needs and gripes. Handle their problems quickly. Call them back immediately if they ask for help, and *keep your promises*. Do all this, and you'll have a happy customer. That's one less cold call you'll have to make for a new or updated product, and one more welcomed hot call.

"For your customers to stay loyal, they have to believe that you're watching out for their interests."

3

Project a Positive Company Image

You might have the best business of its kind in town, but if your premises are messy, your car is always dirty, and your office workers are hurried or rude, then you're not likely to have people beating on your door to do business with you.

Here are some points to check if you want to project a company image that will attract business rather than drive potential clients away at the first point of contact.

✔ **The Telephone**

- **Remember you can't be seen.** Callers have only your voice to guide them, so make sure that it's friendly and that your manner is helpful.

- **Listen carefully and without interruption.** Always have a notepad and pencil on hand to take down the caller's name and telephone number and to record the details of the conversation.

- **Make sure the call is concluded to the satisfaction of the caller.** Did the caller receive the information he or she wanted?

- **Secure an appointment.** Selling is nearly always done face-to-face, so be certain that you say something like, "When may I demonstrate the product for you?"

✔ The Premises

When potential clients get as far as your place of business, make certain that the premises are clean, attractive, and businesslike. File away untidy stacks of magazines or papers, and keep the front counter clean.

✔ The Staff

Dress for the clientele—customers of a CD store featuring rock music will not expect the same dress code as customers of an established financial institution. Your aim should be:

- To dress and groom yourself in a way that will make your clients feel comfortable.

- To be helpful and courteous.

✔ Vehicles

If you have a fleet of company cars, those vehicles are a mobile extension of the company. Executive sedans and company vans should all look as if they are owned by a prosperous, successful organization.

3

Take a Moment...

How's Your Business Image?

Whether you own the business or just work there, you can influence how customers react to it. Check the image of *your* place of work, and ask yourself, *What can I do to help?*

	Poor	Just OK	Good	Very Good	Excellent
Telephone					
• If I were a customer, how would I rate the telephone technique here?	❑	❑	❑	❑	❑
Premises					
• What kind of first impression does the business facility make?	❑	❑	❑	❑	❑
• Is the facility comfortable for clients?	❑	❑	❑	❑	❑
• How would I rate the ease of finding, processing, and delivering information from our office files?	❑	❑	❑	❑	❑
Staff					
• What kind of first impression would the staff's dress and grooming create?	❑	❑	❑	❑	❑
• If I were a client, how would I rate staff courtesy?	❑	❑	❑	❑	❑
Vehicles					
• How do staff vehicles rate in appearance? (Include your private vehicle if you use it for business.)	❑	❑	❑	❑	❑

Finally, complete this sentence:

To help improve my/our business image, I could...

_____

_____

_____

_____

Guard Your Reputation

It's what happens after a sale that builds your reputation. If you really care about your clients, and give them the type of service you'd like yourself, then your reputation will grow and so will your sales. A basic maxim of selling is NO TRUST/NO SALE, and trust develops out of honest, efficient service before and after the sale.

Keep an Eye on Your New Business

An important part of developing an effective prospecting program is to stay aware of the possibilities. To do this, you need to keep easily accessible records of the stages you have reached in your contacts with potential buyers.

- A whiteboard is ideal for keeping a visual record of new and potential sources of business. It can hold press cuttings, business cards, brochures you have collected, and anything that is a guide to a possible sale. Make sure you include an action column to aid your pre-call planning.

- If you are on the road a lot and you feel at home with computers, you might like to work with a personal organizer on a laptop computer. Set it so that reminders pop up about prospective follow-ups.

Telemarketing

These days, wise business professionals can save themselves a lot of effort by using *telemarketing*. Let your fingers do the walking! The chart on the following page offers a six-step guide to telemarketing.

"An important part of developing an effective prospecting program is to stay aware of the possibilities."

A Simple Six-Step Guide to Telemarketing

1. ***Be aware that prospecting is a numbers game.*** You will succeed in getting only a small percentage of prospects to agree to see you. Estimate how many calls you intend to make to predetermine your number of appointments. As a rule of thumb, if you make twenty calls, you can expect to set up two worthwhile appointments *if your telephone technique is effective.*

   • ***Set up a simple, easy-to-read telephone script.*** You'll have to have answers for three standard prospect questions: **Who** are you? **Why** are you calling? and **What** can you do for me?

2. ***Be flexible.*** Having a script in front of you will give you the confidence to become more flexible as you become more experienced. Don't be afraid to try new questions to impress the prospect and improve your overall presentation.

3. ***Stay on track.*** Don't let your prospect's conversation drift into unrelated topics. At the same time, be scrupulously courteous and polite.

4. ***Use customers' names constantly—but not intrusively.*** Many of us have been victims of telemarketers who use our names so often it becomes a joke. "And, Mr. Smith, what's even better…"; "We're sure you'll agree, Mr. Smith, that…"

5. ***Sell yourself.*** Build up feelings of trust and warmth in the listener. Handle objections without too much emotion or drama. Be prepared to listen.

6. ***Sell the appointment, not the product or service.*** You're only trying to get through to the next round. Remember, it's much easier to sell face to face. And don't get discouraged; know that statistics say you'll have to make a lot of telephone calls before winning an appointment.

Chapter Summary

☑ Develop a positive program to seek out and generate new business opportunities. Make sure that when the time to buy comes, prospects include you in the people they turn to.

☑ Maximize the number of referrals to your company by using your personal network. To save yourself time and money, adopt the pre-call planning technique described in this chapter. Do your homework and put yourself in control right at the start of the sales cycle.

☑ Be as visible as possible, so your business is the one clients will seek out. This means advertising, working on your company image, building a reputation for reliability and efficiency, and making sure that you give the best possible after-sales service.

☑ Carefully identify selling possibilities, and then engage in pre-call planning and low-key awareness. Make appointments with the people who make the decisions about what is going to be bought.

CHAPTER FOUR

Step 3: Building Rapport with Prospects

Chapter Objectives

This chapter will help you to:

☑ Identify the factors that will help you build rapport.

☑ Develop the essential skills of effective communication.

☑ Adjust your communication style to your customer.

Nearly every potential buyer will be a stranger to you. However, it's very important that potential clients quickly feel at ease with you and trust you. Only then can you be fairly sure of making a sale. And that's why you need to build **rapport**—that atmosphere of relaxation and trust between people. This makes conversation easy and allows questions to be asked and answered without awkwardness or embarrassment.

But before you tackle the job of building rapport, you must first make sure your communication skills are at their best. Communication is a vital component of building rapport.

Develop Your Communication Skills

These days, most of us learn about basic communication skills in high school. We make presentations as part of our assignments. A career adviser visits our classes to talk about how to communicate with other people, and we learn how to create a good impression in job interviews.

But before you tackle the job of building rapport, you must first make sure your communication skills are at their best. Communication is a vital component of building rapport.

"Show confidence," we hear. *"Make eye contact. Smile. Listen carefully and tell the interviewer what he wants to know, not what you want to tell him. Show interest. Give responses that show you understand what he's saying."*

You're bound to have heard something like this before—if not from a career adviser, then from your parents, or from college lecturers, or from a presenter at an in-house seminar. These are the basic rules of communication in any situation: **show your interest in other people and make them feel important.**

BUT—no matter how many times you've heard all this before, *knowing* it and *doing* it can be two very different things, especially if you've had a long and frustrating day with a string of difficult clients.

4

Communication Skills and Usual Behavior

Spend a few minutes answering the following questions. Examine your communication skills and usual behavior. Do you need to focus a little more on one or two of these areas?

Communication Skills			
	YES	NO	Not Often Enough
1. Do you look customers in the eye?			
2. Do you approach them with a smile?			
3. Do you ask questions that indicate your interest in helping them?			
4. Do you listen to their answers with *real* interest?			
5. Do you respond in such a way that they know you understand their needs?			
6. Do you try to make customers feel important?			

Analyze Your Communication Skills

I make a customer feel at ease by: _____

_____

_____

In my opinion, good listening skills involve: _____

_____

_____

I feel I need to work on the following aspects of communication:

_____

_____

_____

Build Rapport by Searching for Common Links

If rapport is essentially an atmosphere of relaxation and trust between people, then how can we create that trust? Quite simply, trust is based on the things we share with other people. Most of us, when we meet someone new, make an effort to establish a basis for future friendly contacts. We try to open up possible topics of conversation, and we probe for points of contact in our lives. We say things such as:

> "I see from your badge that you are in *(Optimists, Rotary, The Women's Business Club)*. I'm Joanne Brown from the Smithville Club."

This search for common links is a way of establishing the basis for communication. However, to get to the point where people will start to trust you and open up a little, you have to make a good first impression.

4

Make First Impressions Count

Making a good first impression is desirable in any social or business context, but it's especially important in the world of selling. *Research shows that more sales are lost in the first three minutes of contact than at any other time during the whole selling process.* This means that when you meet a potential client, you have to make that person feel at ease with you as soon as possible.

Several factors go into making a good first impression, including your appearance, your basic communication skills, and your overall communication style.

Check Your Appearance

Your appearance speaks for you before you can even say a word. Be sure that yours sends a positive message.

- **Grooming**—Make sure that your hair is neat and appropriately styled and that your clothes are well-pressed. Even if you're one of your company's top salespeople, don't be tempted to rest on your laurels and let your standards slip.

- **Dress**—Avoid extreme styles. Building rapport means making people feel comfortable in your company, so dress fashionably and appropriately for the business you are in.

- **Smile**—A genuine, friendly smile will do more to break the ice than anything else.

Re-check Your Communication Skills

Good communication skills can help you break the ice with even the shyest prospect.

- **Speak First**—Take the initiative; open up the lines of communication. A friendly, pleasant acknowledgment of a customer's presence is enough.

- **Speak Slowly**—If you speak too quickly, people will have trouble understanding you. They'll smile and nod while you talk to them. Then, as you walk away, they'll ask, "What on earth was that all about?"

- **Ask Questions**—It isn't how much you say, or even what you say, that makes you a good conversationalist. It's the questions you ask. Ask questions that are designed to draw answers and establish contact between you and this stranger.

- **Learn To Listen**—Asking questions is the way to get people talking, but it won't work if you don't listen with obvious interest to the response. Good listening involves two basic behaviors.

  — Look at the speaker the entire time he or she is speaking.

  — Provide feedback: Smile, nod, and ask more questions based on what has already been said.

- **Be Positive**—It's very important to project yourself as a positive, optimistic person. To become a better communicator, speak less, listen more, be positive, and ask questions that give people opportunities to talk about themselves.

4

"The key to building rapport is to match your communication style to that of your prospect."

The Key to Building Rapport

The key to building rapport is to match your communication style to that of your prospect. Your communication style consists of many different features, including:

- **Gestures**—one well-timed gesture can mean as much as a five-minute speech.

- **Facial expressions**—the right "look" can stop us dead in our tracks.

- **Silence**—not speaking at all can say far more than the most eloquent speech.

- **Reactivity**—some people are highly reactive; some hardly react at all. Most of us operate somewhere between these two extremes.

Different Customers, Different Styles

Low Reactors use few gestures and speak quietly, with little animation. Don't come on too strong with this type, or they'll sum you up as aggressive and avoid dealing with you.

High Reactors are lively and extroverted. They sound self-assured and use gestures extensively. With this type, make strong eye contact, listen carefully, show interest and understanding in your responses, and project yourself confidently, or they will write you off.

Here are some ways to respond to various communication styles you'll encounter.

- **Copy hand-talkers:** Respond to people who use a lot of gestures by *copying them*. It establishes a sense of affinity.

- **Match energy levels:** If the prospect is a low-energy person and you speak with a lot of energy, you'll wear him or her out. Try to match your expressed energy level to the prospect's.

- **Mimic word pace:** Determine if your prospect is a fast or slow speaker, and mimic his or her word pace. When you do this, listeners subconsciously perceive you to be in tune with them.

If you want to build rapport quickly with people, you have to be able to *match your communication style to the style of your prospect.*

4

Take a Moment...

Take the following True/False quiz on Building Rapport. Suggested answers appear on page 86.

	True	False
1. Most people are highly reactive.	True	False
2. It is possible to vary our communication style according to the situation we are in.	True	False
3. You should respond to "hand-talkers" by mimicking their actions.	True	False
4. The best way to build rapport with someone is to use a complementary style—e.g. if he or she is a low-energy person, you balance that with high-energy reactions.	True	False
5. If you mimic someone's word pace, they will respond to you more readily.	True	False
6. To build rapport means to build trust.	True	False
7. You should approach a prospect as a possible buyer first and as an individual second.	True	False

Chapter Summary

☑ A major problem in the selling situation can be lack of trust. We have to overcome the reservations many people have about professional sellers. Part of the problem is that we all feel a bit awkward when we are dealing with strangers. The simplest solution is to think about how you deal with that in your social life and apply the same principles to business dealings.

☑ Don't approach potential clients only as people who might buy something from you. First acknowledge them as individuals.

☑ Make sure that your prospect recognizes that you are basically a well-intentioned person who is interested in helping him or her.

☑ To establish rapport, you need to build trust and create a comfortable atmosphere in which it is possible to ask questions. The challenge in the world of selling is to do this quickly. So check out your professional image.

- Reflect on your communication skills.

- Develop a positive attitude toward life and the people around you.

☑ Make sure that those first three minutes never cost you a sale.

4

CHAPTER FIVE

Step 4: Exploring Customers' Needs

Chapter Objectives

This chapter will help you to:

- ☑ Prepare for a preliminary interview.

- ☑ Ask the right questions when talking to a prospective buyer.

- ☑ Develop a system for grading the client

How can you improve your sales record? The answer is simple. Talented sellers ask the right questions and listen effectively. That's how they distinguish genuine buyers from the ones who are "just looking." They show customers the products that they *know* will be of interest to them, and they maximize the time spent with people who are likely to buy.

You know the old saying: "You can take a horse to water, but you can't make it drink." You've probably muttered those words yourself at trying times. Well, here's how to deal with an unwilling horse:

1. Make sure the horse is genuinely thirsty.

2. Establish that the horse wants water to drink.

3. Make sure that the horse has access to water displayed to its best advantage.

Under those circumstances, even the most stubborn horse is likely to take a drink. Use that same technique to boost sales. It's based on having the right information about the buyer—and that comes from asking the right questions.

How to Ask the Right Questions

People come to you, the seller, because they have a problem and they hope that you'll be able to help them with it. The best way for you to be able to do that is through a carefully prepared preliminary interview. To obtain the most informative responses from your clients, make sure your questions are open (requiring elaboration by the customer), not closed (requiring only a yes/no answer or a response that locks the client into a position). For example, don't ask *"Are you interested in this model because it's on sale?"* but *"What attracted you to this model?"*

"To obtain the most informative responses from your clients, make sure your questions are open, not closed."

5

Take a Moment...

Convert these Closed Questions to Open Questions. *NOTE: Closed questions require only a yes/no answer and tend to lock the customer into a position. Open questions encourage the customer to elaborate.*

Closed Questions	Open Questions
Do you like this model?	
Were you thinking of buying this for your own use?	
Will you be paying cash for this?	
How much did you want to spend?	
Do you need this product right away?	
Do you need this mainly for word processing?	

Understanding Needs and Motives

The most practical way to maximize the chances of making a sale is to explore your clients' needs and motives. And since all good explorers try to start out with some kind of map, you should do the same. Here's how to "MAP" your clients' needs:

1. **"M" is for Motive**—You need to discover as quickly as possible your client's ***Dominant Buying Motive.*** What might make them think they need your product or service? Ask yourself, "What is this person's ***motive for buying***?" Closely associated with ***Motive*** are clients' ***Expectations***. What do they think they will gain from this purchase?

2. **"A" is for Authority**—The most successful sellers are the people who spend a high proportion of their time with clients who are both *genuinely interested* in making a purchase and who are *able* to make the decision to buy. Ask yourself, "Does this person have the **authority** to make a buying decision?"

3. **"P" is for Price and for Priorities**—You have to know approximately what your client is able to pay for the purchase. Make sure the options you present are within the prospect's means. Ask yourself, "What **price** is this person able to pay?"

   Then take a look at their **Priorities**. How important is this purchase to your client? If they can't get exactly what they want, are they content to wait another six months? How big an impact will the **Price** have on their decision? You need to know this to make a judgement about how much time to spend on your client. Ask yourself, "What are this person's purchasing **priorities**?"

**To be the best explorer in town, simply MAP
your customer's needs:**

M = Motive (and associated expectations)

A = Authority

P = Price and Priorities

Systems Equal Success

Successful explorers keep careful records. If you are going to go to the trouble of "mapping" a client, then that information should be at your fingertips, not just in your head. Don't rely on memory.

Enter your MAP information in a database or a card system, whichever is the most convenient for you to use. Note that person's name, address, and phone number, and record the **Dominant Buying Motive**. Make the entries as soon as possible after contact with the prospect. Then grade the client using this method.

A = buyer is hot

B = buyer is warm

C = buyer is cold

D = buyer is dead

Follow up on the As and Bs and help them make a decision. (No follow up = no sales!) Contact them again at regular intervals. Include contact dates on your system to show the number of times you've called or visited the prospect. A simple guide like this card/computer system puts you in control.

Chapter Summary

☑ Get a pen and a writing pad and write your own set of questions on the basis of the special needs of your industry. Start right now so you can use them tomorrow.

☑ Start a prospect card file or database to help yourself become more organized and more in control of the sales cycle.

☑ Become an explorer in the commercial jungle and "MAP" the results. Your research should open up new areas where focused, informative, and controlled selling can reap far greater financial rewards with less overall time and effort.

☑ Remember, systems equal success.

5

CHAPTER SIX

Step 5: Presenting Your Product Effectively

Chapter Objectives

This chapter will help you to:

☑ Simplify the situation by narrowing the options for a client.

☑ Use the five senses to your advantage in the selling situation.

☑ Make the best use of brochures.

Following the Four Ss

The presentation phase is your chance to make sure that your client really understands what you have to offer. It's a crucial time in the sales process; if you don't get it right, you'll lose the sale. To structure a presentation that really works, follow the four Ss— four simple steps that focus on the customer.

- **Simplify** the choice.
- **Show** the product.
- **Solve** the problems.
- **Sustain** contact.

1. **Simplify the choice.** Don't present your customers with a bewildering range of products that *might* interest them. Don't send them off to explore on their own if they need guidance. Instead, **narrow the range of options** for the buyer. Use your detailed knowledge of your stock or services, and other customers' reactions to it, to make constructive suggestions. **Take clients on a guided tour** of the most appropriate solutions. Your job is to focus the presentation and make it easy for the customer.

2. **Show the customer the product.** You should never *tell* anyone about anything if you can show it to them instead. Your chances of making a sale increase sharply if you allow the customer to interact with the product. Looking and touching are part of that. Depending on the product, hearing, smelling, and tasting might also be appropriate. Humans are sensual beings. Use as many of the five senses as possible to sell your product.

3. **Solve your customers' problems.** If customers express concern about an aspect of the product or service, don't try to persuade them there's nothing to worry about. Let them explore the problem for themselves. Encourage them to ask "What if?" and "What about?" Demonstrate that you understand their concerns, and explain how the product will help to solve their problems. Even better, *show* them how the product will help.

4. **Sustain a relationship with the customer**. Take each customer's name and telephone number, and if possible, let each customer take the product or samples away to try. Offer to find extra information for clients and contact them with that information, or arrange to meet them for a demonstration on site. The important thing is to give clients an obligation to respond in some way.

Your presentation should be structured to require a decision from the buyer. It is quite reasonable to ask the buyer if he or she would like to buy the product you offered or to ask for reasons for rejection.

6

Take a Moment...

Plan a Presentation of Your Product

You have an appointment with a customer to demonstrate/discuss one of your products or services. Fill in the following chart showing how each feature can be presented to the customer as a benefit or an advantage. Use the four Ss to structure your presentation.

Name of Product/Service: _____

Features	Benefits/Advantages to the Customer
1.	1.
2.	2.
3.	3.
4.	4.

I can help the client to visualize/experience the benefits of this product by: _____

_____

_____

Presenting and Using Brochures

There are two types of problems when it comes to using brochures as an aid to sales.

- The brochures are often poorly designed.

- Salespeople rarely know how to use them.

What Are Brochures For?

Scan through a range of brochures. In the majority of cases, the brochure seems to have been produced to make the *company* look good, rather than the product or service. It makes more sense to think about what information a *customer* might find useful. If you have some say in the design of a brochure, **emphasize advantages to the buyer rather than features of the product.**

Customers won't read long passages of text. The information you select should:

- Be carefully selected to emphasize the product's benefits to the customer.

- Be arranged in a format that is easy to read.

- Be brief, preferably in point form.

- Be supplemented by illustrations.

"If you have some say in the design of a brochure, emphasize advantages to the buyer rather than features of the product."

6

How Should Brochures Be Used?

When you hand customers a brochure, you cannot just expect them to read it. For one thing, it might not be easy for them to absorb all the technical detail. For another, your job is to help the customers find answers to their questions. So:

- Get a pen or highlighter and mark the parts of the brochure that answer their questions.

- Encourage customers to interact with the brochure by asking other questions that the brochure can answer.

By the time you've finished, customers should not only know the answers to their questions, but they should be able to return to the brochure at any time and check on the information easily. They should also be able to take the brochure home and discuss all the product benefits with anyone else.

Selling a Service

Selling a service is different from selling a product and therefore the presentation process will be different. A service can't be seen in the same way that a refrigerator can be seen. Your client won't be able to touch it or see how it is functioning. To sell a service, you need to think about what that service *means*.

Consider insurance, for example. You pay for this product, but there's a possibility you might never use it. The more other people use it, the more you have to pay for it. So why do people keep buying insurance?

Because the possibility of loss by fire, theft, or accident is **real to them.** It's **part of their experience.** They have had their car stolen, or they know someone who has. They have read about the devastation caused by house fires. A friend has had his car written off in an accident.

The insurance agent appeals to **self-interest**. When the client can **visualize the service** and **consider its benefits,** you have a strong chance of closing the sale. Use printed materials, audio-visual presentations, and your powers of effective communication to establish the reality of your service in the customer's mind.

Chapter Summary

☑ The way you present your product to your clients is of critical importance in the sales cycle.

☑ What you show should come from what you have learned during the exploring phase. Your aim is to promote easy communication and to make it simple for your clients to understand what your product has to offer them.

☑ Any product brochures or sales material must be easily understood by the customer. Walk through the material while you have the customer's attention.

☑ If you are selling a service, you must **make the service appear as tangible as possible.** Make sure the service matches the expectations you developed.

☑ To ensure your personal success in the presentation round of the sales cycle, I suggest you follow the four simple Ss that focus on the customer: **Simplify** the choice, **Show** the product, **Solve** problems, and **Sustain** contact.

6

CHAPTER SEVEN

Step 6: Handling Customers' Objections

Chapter Objectives

This chapter will help you to:

☑ Analyze objections to find out what the client really wants.

☑ Use the six-step method of handling objections.

☑ Resolve objections and move on to close the sale.

The Welcome Truth about Objections

One of the greatest problems we have in the sales process is that we tend to take objections personally. We allow ourselves to become discouraged by an objection. We can even believe it marks the end of the deal. But we couldn't be more wrong.

An objection is not something to worry about. It's a sign that the prospect is showing real interest. Let's list the reasons why objections are a positive part of the sales process.

1. Objections demonstrate the buyer's interest.

2. Objections bring the buyer's thoughts and feelings out into the open where you can deal with them.

3. Objections provide you with feedback by showing what the buyer thought you said.

4. Objections give you the opportunity to provide additional service or guidance.

"An objection is not something to worry about. It's a sign that the prospect is showing real interest."

What Does an Objection Mean to You?

Before reading the rest of this chapter, take a moment to focus on your own feelings about customers' objections and your methods of handling them.

When a customer raises objections to the sale, I feel _____

_____

_____.

I handle objections by _____

_____

_____.

I think most customers raise objections because _____

_____

_____.

Objections are an important part of the sales cycle. They are an indication that a potential client has a problem that needs solving. By thinking of yourself as a problem solver, you can use all the clues offered by prospects to help them find solutions. Be alert for such clues in the form of:

- Critical comments about the range of products they've seen so far.
- Reasons for deferring a decision to buy.

Working through objections is probably the only real way you can find out what's going on in your customers' heads. What you need is a system that will help you:

- Deal with the prospect's objections.
- Use those objections to help you finalize the sale.

The following is one such system which works well.

7

Six Steps in Handling Objections

Listen

Encourage your prospect to talk and take careful note of what he or she says.

Respond to the Objection

Let your prospect know that you understand what he or she is saying and that you take that concern seriously. Try restating what has been said to show you understand the objection, or respond with comments such as "I see what you mean" or "I understand what you're getting at." Aim for a **neutral response**, free of emotion or judgement.

Categorize the Objection

Not every objection deserves a serious response. You can let a trivial objection pass without any attention, but you're in trouble if you ignore important objections. How can you tell which objections are important? Usually by using your common sense. For example, for a real estate sales person, *"I don't like the wallpaper in that bedroom"* is trivial; *"I don't like the neighborhood"* is important. The first problem can be changed; the second can't.

Respond Promptly

When you decide that an objection deserves attention, respond at once. If you don't, your prospect will think you're being evasive and will keep coming back to that same point.

The prospect will also think you're incompetent because you can't give a prompt, reasonable reply to a serious objection.

Deal with the Objection

Once you're sure the objection is important and you've shown the prospect that you understand what he or she has said, you're ready to deal with it. The following list of DOs and DON'Ts offers you a set of rules for dealing with objections effectively.

DOs	DON'Ts
• Remain positive.	• Be defensive and irritable.
• Show interest and listen carefully.	• Display indifference and boredom.
• Re-phrase the objector's response.	• Allow the prospect to feel that you're not taking him or her seriously.
• Keep control of yourself and the discussion.	• Talk too much or argue with the prospect.
• Probe for further information with questions.	• Try to answer irrelevant objections.
• Allow the prospect to answer his/her own questions and find his/her own solutions.	• Respond to objections with, "Yes, but…" or interrupt the prospect.
• Show how the objection is outweighed by the advantages the product offers.	• Magnify the importance of the objection by overreacting.
• Be precise in your response.	• Hurry your response.

7

> **"The feel/felt/found method allows you to introduce another point of view in a discussion without openly disagreeing with the prospect's."**

Use the Feel/Felt/Found Method of Responding to Objections

The feel/felt/found method allows you to introduce another point of view in a discussion without openly disagreeing with the prospect. For example, in reply to an objection by a prospect about using your company's accounting service, you could say,

*I understand why you **feel** that way. Others have **felt** the same, but they have **found** that there are special benefits in using our personalized and highly specialized accounting service.*

Resolve the Issue and Move On

You've dealt with the objection, but is the prospect satisfied? Don't move on if the prospect is still uneasy about some aspect of the issue. It might become a sore point if you neglect to clear it up completely. Try to focus on the precise nature of your customer's problem. You might say something like,

I can see that you're still not certain about the price. About how much did you wish to pay?

OR

I can see that you're still concerned about the location of this house. Could you tell me exactly what's worrying you?

Make sure the objection has been dealt with by asking, "Does that seem all right to you?" or "Are you happy with that?"

Chapter Summary

☑ Objections are clues to what the buyer really needs or wants.

☑ Objections are a natural part of selling. Don't take them personally. They're a sign of interest. No interest = no reaction.

☑ Remember that dealing with objections is just another aspect of communication with the client. Refer to the other chapters that deal explicitly with different aspects of communication.

☑ Be a problem solver. Listen closely, and, like Sherlock Holmes, use the clues on objections to help turn a negative reaction into a point of agreement. Apply the feel/felt/found system explained in this chapter. You will improve greatly with practice.

7

CHAPTER EIGHT

Step 7: Testing Customers' Reactions During the Sale

Chapter Objectives

This chapter will help you to:

☑ Obey the unstated rule of polite conversation.

☑ Ask key questions to test client reactions and help customers sell themselves.

☑ Understand the Road Rules of the Testing Phase.

Testing, Testing...

It has been said that successful salespeople know their ABCs—"Always Be Closing." I see serious difficulties with this approach. If you try to close the sale too early, or at the wrong moment, you can find yourself back where you started. You will have to re-establish rapport, explore the buyer's needs again, and so on. That isn't just irritating, it might mean that your customer's trust in you collapses. So let's replace ABC with ABT —"Always Be Testing." This is an important distinction.

Remember that selling is an act of communication. It involves a two-way flow of information: speaking and listening. It's easy for a seller to come on too strong, to act as the powerful person in the interaction with the customer. Some salespeople are constantly informing, advising, and directing. They continue to press for a decision when anyone with any sense would notice that the other person just wants to escape.

"Remember that selling is an act of communication."

Good communication is a cooperative act. Make sure you allow the client to participate. You *do* have to close the sale. But an obsession with closing at all stages can cause you to break an unstated rule of polite conversation: *speak, listen,* then *respond.* **Keep the dialogue open by asking for the customer's FEELINGS, OPINIONS, and REACTIONS.**

Take a Moment...

The unstated rules of conversation may be summarized as "Speak, Listen, Respond."

What does this mean to you?_____

_____

_____

What Types of Questions Should You Ask?

In Step 4, you asked questions to establish your client's needs. The information you learned helped you to present your product effectively. Now that you're at the testing phase of the selling process, you will want to ask the kinds of questions that help clients to think things through for themselves. Your questions can bring to the surface anything that might be blocking the sale. By answering your questions, clients can literally talk themselves into buying.

8

What types of questions should you ask? Some examples are:

- How do you feel about this product?
- How useful do you think it will be for you?
- What do you like about it?
- What do you dislike?
- What do you think?

As the conversation continues, your questions should become more specific.

- How do you think it compares with competing products?
- What do you think would be the major benefits of buying this product?
- What reservations do you have about this product?

You are **testing** the customer's response to the product. And as the customer answers, you will learn which of your product's benefits to highlight. But beware! Don't keep jumping in to contradict what the customer is saying.

The Road Rules of the Testing Phase

STOP • LOOK • LISTEN

- When you have asked the testing question, STOP.

- While the customer is talking, LOOK. Attend to body language. Look at the customer's face. Take note of whether the customer is looking at you or at the floor. This will give you the best information about your client's emotions.

- Don't just hear what your customer is saying, LISTEN. Use what you learn to decide what you have to do next. Show active interest and understanding. Nod, smile, and ask intelligent questions that show you understand your customer's concerns. No one has ever listened him- or herself out of a sale.

Keep them talking. While they're talking, they're actually selling to themselves. To keep them talking use a statement like, "Would you expand on that?" or "Would you take that one step further?"

8

Take a Moment...

Fill in answers to the following questions.

1. Why is it important to explore the client's needs?

   _____

   _____

   _____

2. What is most likely to earn you a rejection?

   _____

   _____

   _____

3. What are the best kinds of questions to ask in relation to the product?

   _____

   _____

   _____

4. Why is it important to let the client talk?

   _____

   _____

   _____

Chapter Summary

✔ When you've reached the testing phase of the sales cycle, your job is 80% done. If you've:

- Established rapport properly;
- Explored the customer's needs carefully;
- Presented purchasing options which are genuinely able to satisfy their needs; and
- Dealt honestly with their objections,

then the testing phase will take you to the threshold of the sale.

✔ Most people find decision-making difficult, especially when it means parting with money. Getting through this reluctance barrier is a crucial part of the sales cycle.

✔ Your aim should be to test the customer with options that lead him or her through the decision-making process, so that the final step of actually making the purchase follows easily and naturally from what has gone before.

✔ Testing goes well beyond dealing with objections. Through questioning, it focuses attention on any barrier to purchasing. It invites clients to talk through their problems so the final decision is easier to make.

8

CHAPTER NINE

Step 8: Closing the Sale

Chapter Objectives

This chapter will help you to:

☑ Understand the general principles of closing a sale

☑ Use different types of closes to suit individual clients

What is actually involved in closing a sale? There is no single answer to that question, but here are some general principles:

Ask for the Business

If you don't ask, you won't sell. Ask for your customer's business every time.

Believe in Your Product

You have to believe in your product, and you have to believe that it's right for the customer. If you are selling a well-made product with excellent backup services, belief is easy. So **find a product you can believe in**. And if you really can't believe in your product, **FIND ANOTHER PRODUCT TO SELL!** It's a simple matter of survival.

> **As a seller your job is clear:**
>
> - You must know your product as well as you possibly can.
>
> - You must believe in the advantages it will offer buyers, and you must sell those advantages to them.
>
> - You don't have to believe that your product is perfect. But you do have to believe that it has something special to offer.

Concentrate on Communication

Selling is an act of communication. And communication requires concentration so that you can respond appropriately to special circumstances.

Remember you are dealing with human beings, not machines. Human beings vary from one moment to the next in the way they respond to people and circumstances. If you want to be a seller who is a cut above the rest, you will have to become an expert at *concentration* and *response*.

Evaluate the Situation

If you have concentrated, listened, and watched, you will know when your clients feel that all their problems and questions have been dealt with and answered. That's the moment when you should move to close the sale. If you leave it hanging, even for a little while, the mood might change and the sale could be lost.

9

Take a Moment...

Take the following True/False quiz on Closing the Sale. Suggested answers appear on page 86.

1. You should never pressure a customer by asking for the sale.	**True**	**False**
2. If you don't believe in your product, you should find another product to sell	**True**	**False**
3. It's OK to sell the advantages of a product to a customer even if you don't think it's right for them—a sale is a sale.	**True**	**False**
4. When you've been in sales a while, you can accurately predict a customer's responses.	**True**	**False**
5. Knowing when to close the sale is largely the result of being alert and responsive to the customer.	**True**	**False**
6. It isn't necessary to believe that your product has something special to offer your customers to sell it to them.	**True**	**False**

Different Types of Closes

Good sellers are good observers of human beings. They learn to recognize personality types and the types of approaches that suit each type. Here are some examples of different types of closes and the people they suit.

- **Direct Close**—If you can tell from a person's responses that you've made a sale, it's time to secure it. Simply ask directly for the sale. For example, *"Well, it's clear that Product X is the perfect solution to your needs. Why don't you let me take care of the details, and you can take it home with you?"*

- **Alternative Choice Close**—Some people have to feel that they are in absolute control. If the seller is too direct they become suspicious and even hostile. With people like that, you have to be sure they feel the final decision is theirs and theirs alone. When the moment is right, you might say something like, "We've looked at a number of products which will solve your problems. They're all excellent value for the money. Which one do you believe is right for you?"

- **Summary Close**—Use this close with customers who like to consider all the facts and pride themselves on making a logical decision. Give these clients as much information as they want. When you sense that the moment is right, summarize the facts, emphasizing the aspects of the product that most interested them. Then, ask for the sale.

- **Double Close**—This close works for clients who have agreed to buy, then show some doubt that they've made the right decision. The double close is a simple reassurance that they've made a good purchase. You'll say something like, "You've done well. You won't regret buying this," OR "This is perfect for you." Only use this close if you really believe that the customer has done well. Insincerity is transparent and can make a contented buyer nervous once more.

9

Take a Moment...

In the left-hand column are four different types of closes. In the right-hand column, describe the type of client they suit.

Type of Close	Suited to What Type of Client?
Direct Close	
Alternative Choice Close	
Summary Close	
Double Close	

Chapter Summary

☑ If you can't close, you can't sell. Closing is an art. It is listening, talking, observing, and above all, being ready to ask for your customer's business as you near the end of the sales cycle.

☑ The key to closing is to listen to the buying signals your client is giving out: a statement, a gesture, a nod. The clue can be verbal or nonverbal. Once you've identified the signals, don't be afraid to move in for the close.

☑ "Closing" is really the start of more sales. It's part of the sales cycle, and cycles keep going around endlessly, like a carousel. You have established a new business relationship, and that adds another segment to the growing network of contacts for you, the seller. Whenever you close a sale, don't think "Well, that's another one finished." Instead, you should think, "Well, let's see what can be built on that foundation."

9

Step 9: Delivering Outstanding After-Sales Service

Chapter Objectives

This chapter will help you to:

☑ Understand the two Rs that hold up your business.

☑ Initiate an after-sales service/contact plan.

The Three Most Important Selling Words

Three of the most important selling words in the '90s are: **trust, integrity, value**. Burn them into your brain. Build these concepts into everything you do.

Building trust with clients is pretty simple, really. All you need to do is make good on what you *say* you will do. Call back on time. Deliver on time. Give customers the facts. And finally, follow up with quality after-sales service to *show* you care. Outstanding after-sales service is one of the things that really singles out the superior seller. The benefits to you? Your sales career will be secure when your customers keep coming back to buy again.

Take a Moment...

After-Sales Service

What does After-Sales Service mean to you? _____

_____

_____

_____

_____

_____

(Refer to this after you have read the rest of the chapter. See if you still hold the same views. Is there anything you want to change or add?)

Characteristics of An Effective After-Sales Contact Plan

- You have a standard procedure for communicating with clients after the sale.

- You contact past buyers at least twice a year.

- You have a system for maintaining contacts established through sales.

- You demonstrate a strong commitment to solving problems connected with the product after the sale.

- You regard after-sales service as part of the sales process rather than an optional extra.

10

The Two Rs

A large part of your success as a seller will hinge on two Rs—**return sales** and **referrals**. Good after-sales service contributes to the development of both. Think of it like this: making a sale establishes a relationship. If clients buy from you, they probably trust you. It would be a big mistake to let them forget you, especially when it takes only a little effort and organization to maintain contact.

In general, after-sales service is common sense and should become second nature to any salesperson. It is the key to a long life in selling. To be successful at after-sales service, you need to set up a system in which the people who have bought from you hear from you again and again.

Setting Up an After-Sales Service System

There are a number of inexpensive ways to maintain contact and trust. For example, you could:

- Write a letter.

- Call and say "hi."

- Telephone to see how the product/service is going.

- Send something like the latest brochure in the mail.

- Send out holiday/birthday cards.

- Buy some small giveaway item to keep your client base stimulated.

After-sales service means looking after your clients' needs and solving their problems after the point of sale. It means that you consider the service to be part of the product. You're not just selling an insurance policy. You're also making sure that claims are processed and paid promptly. You're not just shampooing carpets. You're also putting the furniture back where it came from and telephoning the next day to see if the customer is happy with the job.

> **"After-sales service means looking after your clients' needs and solving their problems after the point of sale."**

Never forget that when you are dealing with a customer, you are dealing with his or her perception of you. Maybe the problem wasn't your fault or you honestly didn't know the product was faulty, or unavailable. It doesn't matter. All the excuses under the sun won't make the customer believe in you again, unless you do something to put it right.

Ask yourself:

- Do I strive to justify the customer's trust in me on every occasion?

- If something goes wrong, do I admit the mistake and take immediate steps to rectify it and offer something new?

- Do I give good value to my customer for his or her investment of time, energy, and money?

If you can answer yes to these three questions, you're ready to sail into selling success in the '90s fortified by the trust placed in you by your customers.

Take a Moment...

List some of the ways you could maintain contact with the customers in your line of business.

1. _____

_____

_____

2. _____

_____

_____

3. _____

_____

_____

4. _____

_____

_____

5. _____

_____

_____

What is the first step you would take in maintaining better contact with your existing customers? _____

_____

_____

_____

Chapter Summary

☑ If you don't make a deliberate attempt to sustain your relationships with past buyers, you'll lose them. And that should be a matter of serious concern to you. If you don't maintain the old contacts while you make new ones, there will be no growth and development in your career.

☑ After-sales service brings you return sales and referrals.

☑ After-sales service isn't just an optional extra. It has to be an essential part of your approach to selling if you truly want to succeed.

☑ After-sales service can include follow-up letters and telephone calls, brochures related to the product, Christmas and Easter cards, handouts on getting the best out of a product, occasional newsletters, and special service offers.

Conclusion

This book contains lots of ideas and advice about improving yourself and your selling techniques. But in the end, the only one who can make a difference is *you*.

For selling to be both rewarding and easy, you have to find a way to maintain your enthusiasm about the selling you do. The best way to do this is to find a *mentor*.

Finding a Mentor

Your mentor should be someone you can look up to yet relate to. Who in your local community or line of business would you most like to emulate? When you know the answer to that question, take a simple, positive step. Call or write to that person. All you have to do is say you'd like to meet that person or buy him or her lunch.

Be honest with your prospective mentor about your motivation. Tell him or her you are looking for **encouragement** and **direction**. The real movers and shakers have no problems with sharing their knowledge. Chances are, they've been where you are and someone else helped them get started.

You could well be starting a relationship or network of contacts that will change your selling life forever. A mentor has one great asset to share—*sales experience*.

When you speak and listen to a mentor, you'll probably find that there are four major MUST-DOs which that person has found to be of benefit over the years.

The Mentor's Must-Do List

- Adopt a positive mindset.
- Realize that school is never out.
- Set a yearly personal goal for what you're selling.
- Make yourself do the things you don't want to do.

1. **Adopt a positive mindset**. The first thing that should strike you about the person you're working with is his or her positive attitude (otherwise you've picked the wrong mentor). A positive mindset is as contagious as the flu. Drop your immune system and try to catch it, then try it on your clients and prospects.

2. **Realize that school is never out**. Find out more about how your mentor keeps up-to-date with his or her business. This may range from reading the latest books on improving selling techniques to attending classes. The golden rule is never stop educating yourself. Remember that you can learn from more than one mentor. Any mentor who doesn't keep up to date will quickly fall to the back of the pack, regardless of past successes.

3. **Set a personal yearly sales goal**. Successful people rarely make it by accident. Planning how to achieve a particular goal has always been a critical part of the process. Be **specific** and **personalize** your sales goal. Think in terms of what size sales goal you can reasonably achieve through the coming year. Then increase it by 10 percent, just to make your goal worth striving for. As each month passes, draw up a quick bar graph to show your sales progress. This will serve as a constant reminder of what you have achieved.

4. **Make yourself do things you don't want to do**. Remember how as children we always had to eat our vegetables before we even looked at dessert? The principle is the same in sales—you've got to find that special reward to make yourself do the things you don't want to do.

   Talk to anybody. No matter how successful they are, they all have something they dislike doing. They don't let it get the better of them, and you shouldn't either. Don't put unpleasant tasks off—get rid of them.

"Be specific and personalize your sales goal."

Self-Check: An Overview of Successful Selling

Complete the statements below.

1. I plan to improve the organization of my day by...

   _____

   _____

   _____

2. My personal network will benefit my sales career in this way:

   _____

   _____

   _____

3. In my opinion, the three most important factors in building rapport are:

   1. _____

   2. _____

   3. _____

4. The difference between closed and open questions is...

   _____

   _____

   _____

5. The two main problems with using brochures as an aid to sales are...

   1. _____

   2. _____

Self-Check: An Overview of Successful Selling *(Cont.)*

6. Objections are a positive part of the sales process because...

_____

_____

_____

7. The Road Rules of the Testing Phase are Stop, Look, and Listen. This means...

_____

_____

_____

8. It is important to believe in the product you sell because...

_____

_____

_____

9. The Selling Words of the '90s are Trust, Integrity, and Value. These concepts are important because...

_____

_____

_____

10. The advantage of having a mentor is...

_____

_____

_____

Chapter 4
Take a Moment ... *(page 44)*
1. **False.** Most people fall somewhere in between high reactors and low reactors.
2. **True.**
3. **True.**
4. **False.** You should try to match that person's style.
5. **True.**
6. **True.**
7. **False.** You should approach everyone as an individual first.

Chapter 9
Take a Moment ... *(page 72)*
1. **False.** You should ask for your customer's business every time.
2. **True**
3. **False.** You have to believe that the product you are selling is right for your customer.
4. **False.** Everyone is different, and it is difficult to predict a customer's response.
5. **True**
6. **False.** You don't have to believe that your product is perfect, but you do have to believe it has something special to offer.

NOTES

NOTES